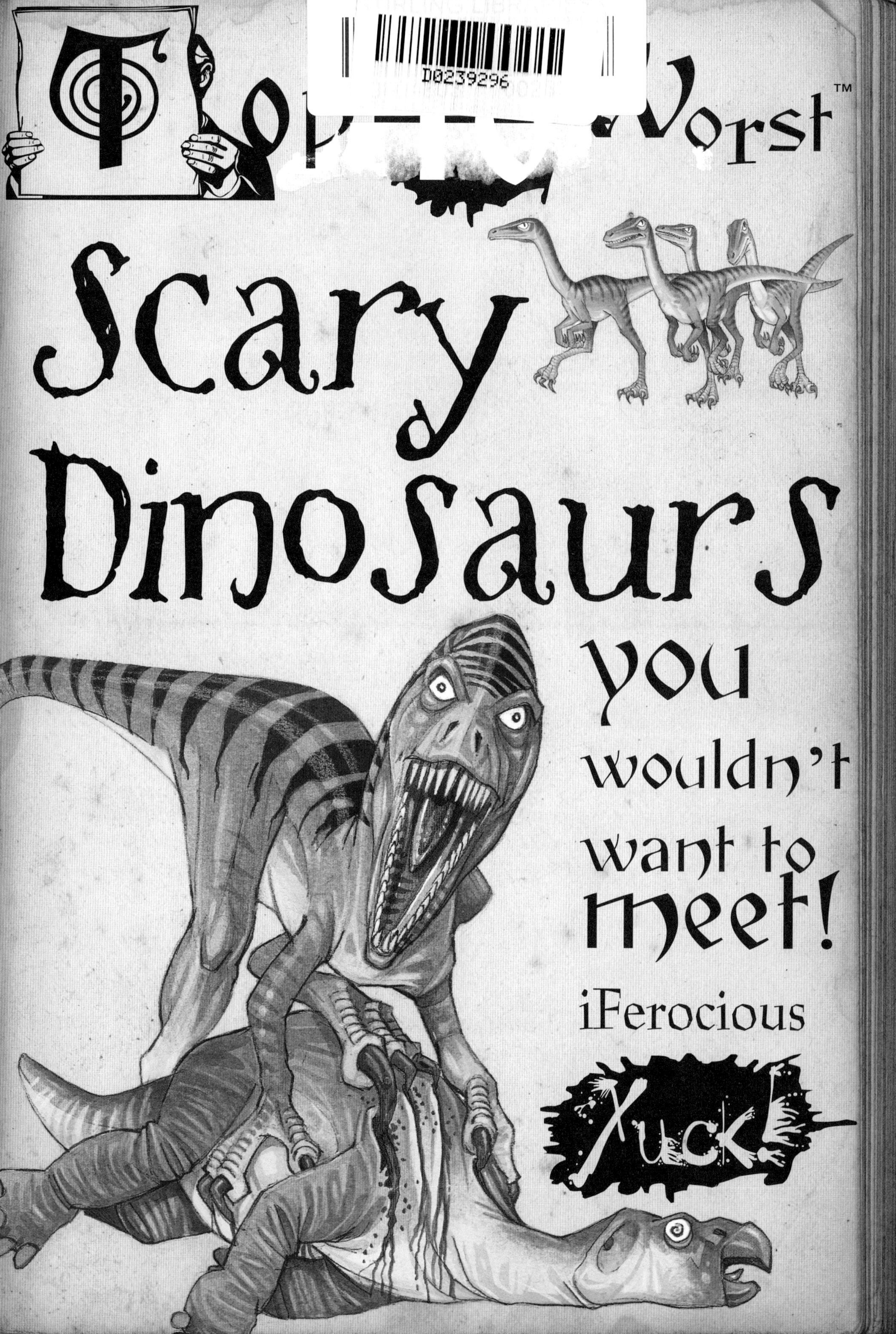
Top 10 Worst™
Scary Dinosaurs
you wouldn't want to meet!
iFerocious
Yuck!
D0239296

Author:
Carolyn Franklin graduated from Brighton College of Art with a focus on design and illustration. Since then she has worked in animation, advertising, and children's fiction and non-fiction. She has a special interest in natural history and has written many books on the subject.

Scientific Consultant:
John Cooper

Artist:
David Antram was born in Brighton, England, in 1958. He studied at Eastbourne College of Art and then worked in advertising for fifteen years before becoming a full-time artist. He has illustrated many children's non-fiction books.

Series creator:
David Salariya was born in Dundee, Scotland. He has illustrated a wide range of books and has created and designed many new series for publishers in the UK and overseas. In 1989 he established The Salariya Book Company. He lives in Brighton with his wife, illustrator Shirley Willis, and their son Jonathan.

Additional artists: Nick Hewetson, Carolyn Scrace

Editor: Jamie Pitman

Editorial assistant: Mark Williams

Visit our website at **www.book-house.co.uk**
or go to **www.salariya.com** for
free electronic versions of:

You Wouldn't Want to be an Egyptian Mummy!
You Wouldn't Want to be a Roman Gladiator!
You Wouldn't Want to be a Polar Explorer!
You Wouldn't Want to Sail on a 19th-Century Whaling Ship!

Printed and bound in China.

Published in Great Britain in MMX by
Book House, an imprint of
The Salariya Book Company Ltd
25 Marlborough Place, Brighton BN1 1UB
www.salariya.com
www.book-house.co.uk

HB ISBN-13: 978-1-907184-46-8
PB ISBN-13: 978-1-907184-47-5

SALARIYA

1 3 5 7 9 8 6 4 2
A CIP catalogue record for this book is available from the British Library.

PAPER FROM SUSTAINABLE FORESTS

Top 10 Worst™

Scary Dinosaurs

you wouldn't want to meet!

Illustrated by
David Antram

Written by
Carolyn Franklin

Created & designed by
David Salariya

Contents

The age of dinosaurs

For over 160 million years during the Mesozoic Era, dinosaurs were the dominant creatures on Earth. These incredible creatures became extinct 65 mya (million years ago). Dinosaurs were prehistoric reptiles and most of them hatched from eggs. The ten scary dinosaurs in this book were all fearsome killers, but for ten very different reasons.

In the beginning!

All the animals below are related to each other. Dinosaurs, such as the three on this page, evolved from a group of primitive reptiles, which were related to present day crocodiles. Deinonychus belonged to a group of amazing dinosaurs that could be the ancestors of modern birds.

Pteranodon was a flying reptile, but not a dinosaur!
Wingspan: 7.6 m (25 ft)
Lived: 85-64 mya

Diplodocus
Length: 26 m (85 ft)
Lived: 155-145 mya

Modern pigeon
Wingspan: 30 cm (12 inches)

Deinonychus
Length: 3 m (10 ft)
Lived: 120-110 mya

Modern crocodile
Length: 3-4.6 m (10-15 ft)

Stegosaurus
Length: 6-7.5 m (20-25 ft)
Lived: 150-140 mya

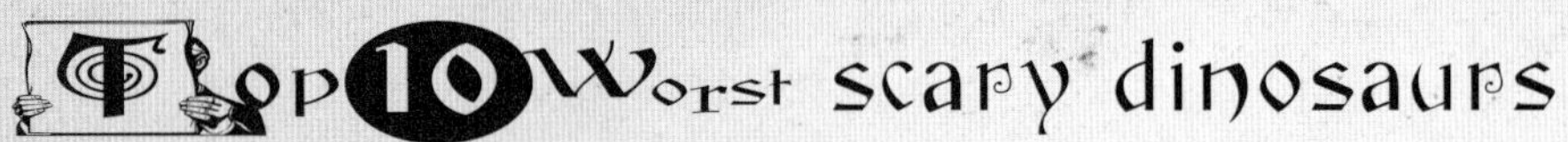

All shapes and sizes!

There were many different types of dinosaur. Some lived in extremely hot and cold habitats, and had to adapt to the environment in order to survive. Varying greatly in size, some were the largest animals to ever walk on Earth, whereas others were no bigger than a chicken. While many dinosaurs were able to run fast, others were slow and lumbering. Some walked on two legs, others on four, and some dinosaurs could even do both.

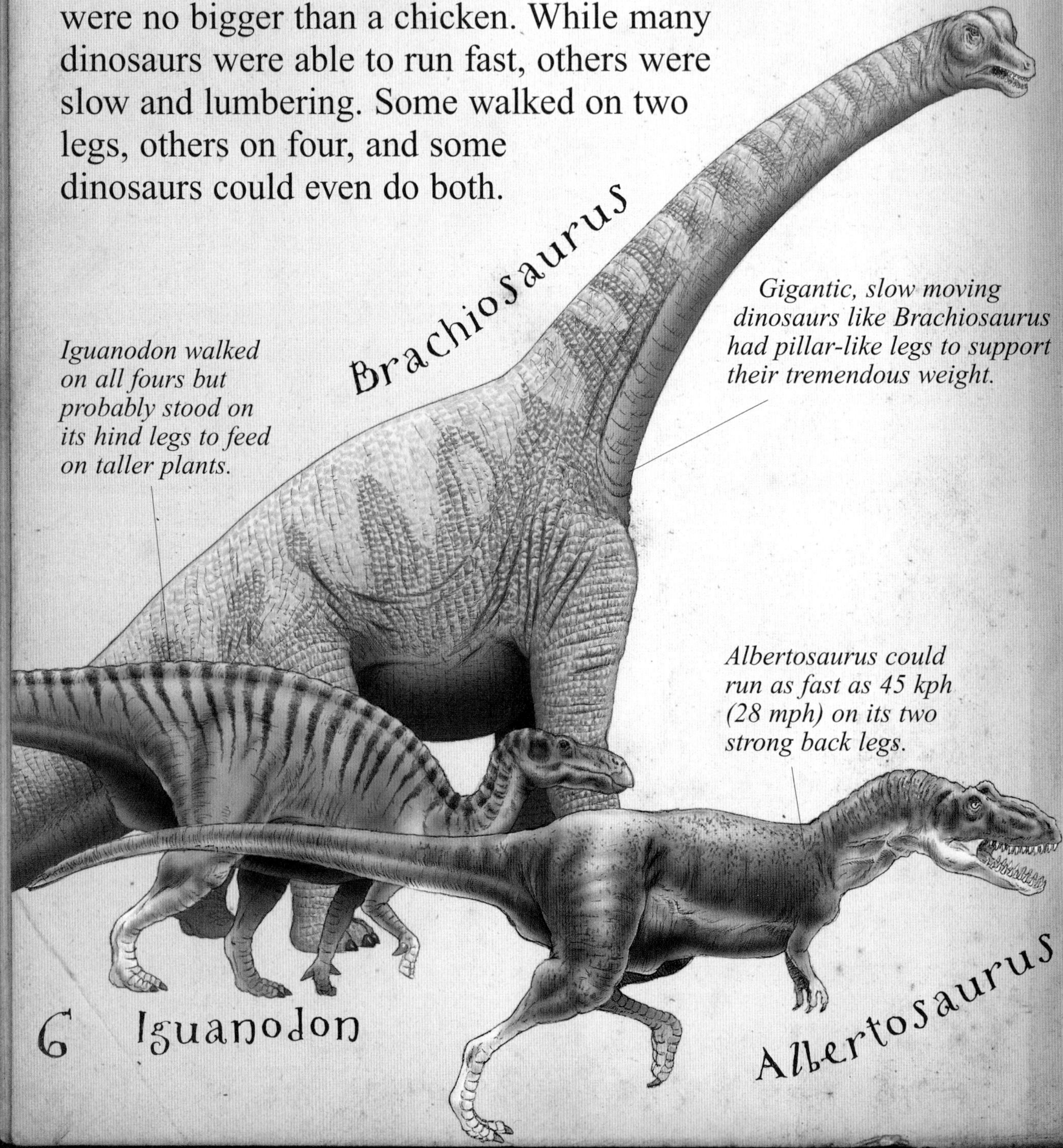

Brachiosaurus

Gigantic, slow moving dinosaurs like Brachiosaurus had pillar-like legs to support their tremendous weight.

Iguanodon walked on all fours but probably stood on its hind legs to feed on taller plants.

Albertosaurus could run as fast as 45 kph (28 mph) on its two strong back legs.

Iguanodon

Albertosaurus

Mesozoic era

No one type of dinosaur lasted for the whole of the Mesozoic Era. They evolved during the Triassic Period (227-205 mya), and lived through the Jurassic and Cretaceous Periods (205-65 mya). Then, towards the end of the Cretaceous Period, they became extinct. Dinosaurs were constantly evolving, and the first dinosaurs that appeared in the early Jurassic Period were mostly very different from those still alive at the end of the Cretaceous Period.

End of the Cretaceous Period (65 mya)

Modern fish, flowering plants and birds evolve.

Start of the Cretaceous Period (144 mya)

The end of the Jurassic Period. The last dinosaurs evolve.

Start of the Jurassic Period (205 mya)

Many of the largest dinosaurs evolve.

Dinosaurs are widespread on the supercontinent.

Start of the Triassic Period (227 mya)

The first dinosaurs evolve.

The time spiral of the Mesozoic era starts at the bottom, showing the earth 225 mya. It winds upwards showing the different periods when the dinosaurs evolved. It stops around 65 mya when the dinosaurs and many other prehistoric animals died out.

Were all dinosaurs scary?

The majority of dinosaurs were herbivores (plant-eaters) and omnivores (plant and meat-eaters). However, the remaining dinosaurs were bloodthirsty, flesh-eating carnivores!

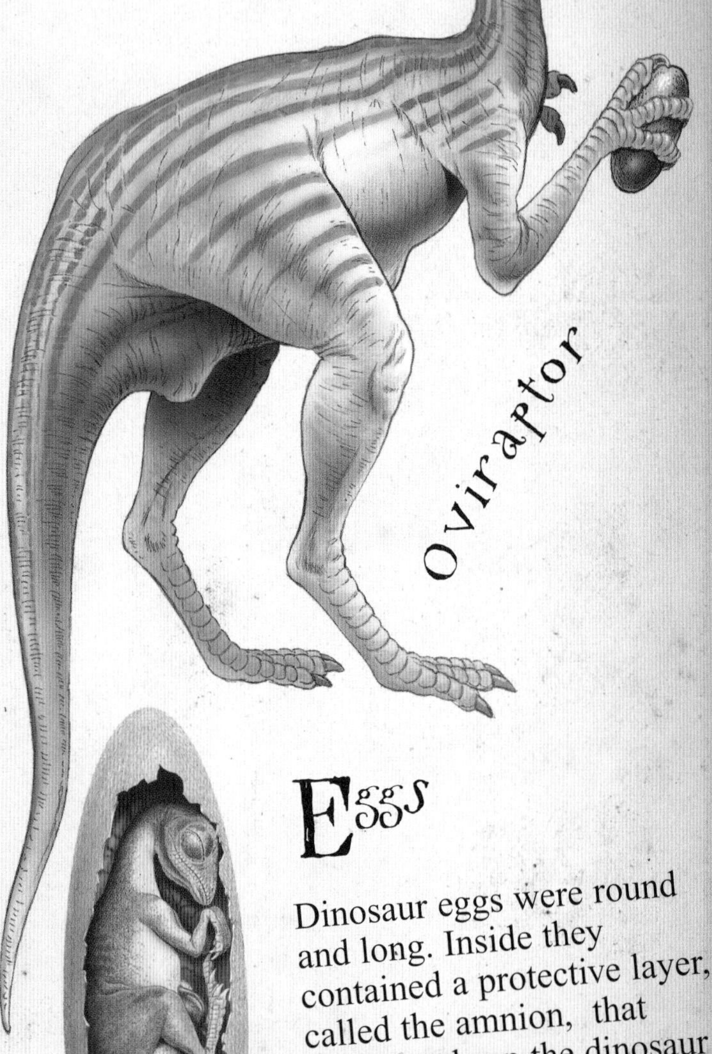

Fast food

Oviraptor, a small omnivorous dinosaur, had a parrot-like head, a short, toothless beak and very powerful jaws. Its diet consisted of meat, eggs, seeds, insects and plants. Oviraptor had two long, thin, bird-like legs and it could run up to 70 kph (43 mph), which is as fast as an ostrich living in the present day.

Found innocent

Palaeontologists found a fossilised Oviraptor on top of some dinosaur eggs, and for many years they believed that the Oviraptor had been eating them. Later evidence showed that the Oviraptor was actually a parent of the eggs in the nest, and not an egg thief after all!

Eggs

Dinosaur eggs were round and long. Inside they contained a protective layer, called the amnion, that helped to keep the dinosaur embryo moist.

Embryo

Amnion

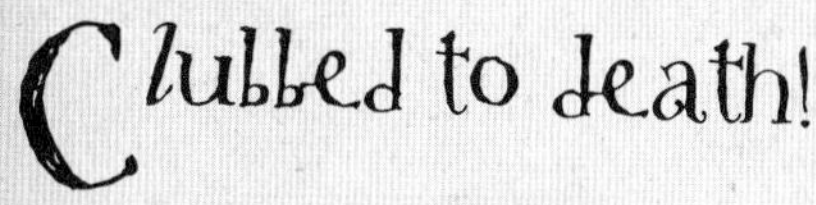

Clubbed to death!

Despite their peaceful diet of plants, many of the herbivores had fiendish ways of defending themselves against bloodthirsty carnivores. Euoplocephalus was a large herbivorous dinosaur which was covered in armour for protection. It also had rows of large spikes along its body and horns on its head. Its club-like tail was its secret weapon, and would have been a useful defence even against a hungry Tyrannosaurus.

Killing machines

Carnivorous dinosaurs were designed to kill! Most had long, strong legs so they could run fast to chase their prey. Large, powerful jaws equipped with sharp, pointed teeth, and claws for killing and tearing the flesh of their prey completed this lethal combination.

No 10

Masiakasaurus

A bipedal dinosaur with a long neck and tail, Masiakasaurus had one extraordinary feature – its terrifying teeth. Its long, sharp front teeth pointed forward, which is rare for predatory dinosaurs. Its vicious lower front teeth were almost horizontal, and would have been ideal for spearing prey. Its blade-like back teeth cut and ripped its victim's flesh into tasty, bite-sized chunks.

Vital statistics

Name:	Masiakasaurus (mah-shee-ah-kah-SORE-us)
Meaning:	Vicious lizard
Length:	Up to 2 m (6 ft)
Weight:	35 kg (77 lb)
Diet:	Carnivorous
Time span:	84-71 mya
Period:	Late Cretaceous
Found:	Madagascar

You wouldn't want to know this:

A piece of fossilised dinosaur dung is called a coprolite and it can tell us how, who and what the dinosaur ate!

Masiakasaurus' diet consisted of fish, lizards and other, smaller dinosaurs.

Be prepared! Always expect to read the very worst

Dinosaur teeth

Scientists studying a dinosaur's fossilised teeth can discover what it ate, how it got the food, and whether it chewed, crushed, or just swallowed it whole! Teeth are harder than bone and fossilise more easily. This is how we know that some dinosaurs existed even though only their teeth remain.

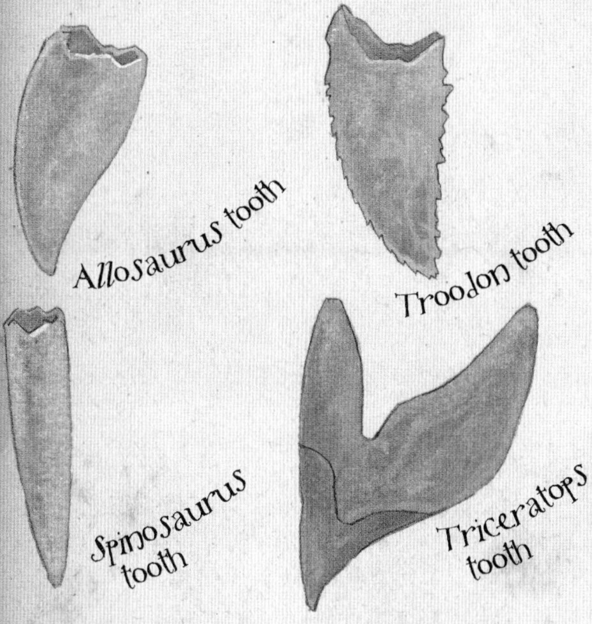

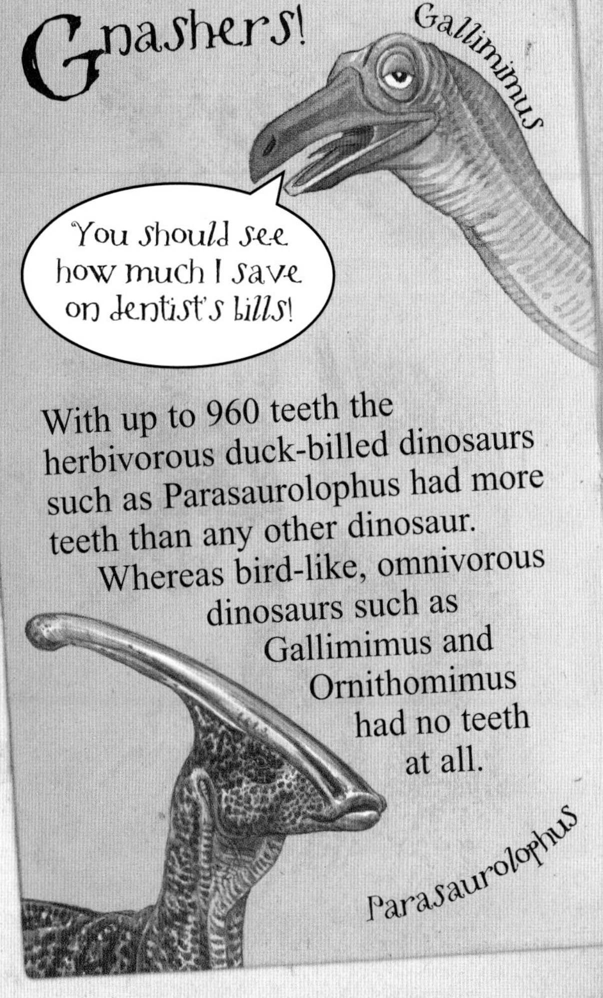

With up to 960 teeth the herbivorous duck-billed dinosaurs such as Parasaurolophus had more teeth than any other dinosaur. Whereas bird-like, omnivorous dinosaurs such as Gallimimus and Ornithomimus had no teeth at all.

Fierce carnivores like Allosaurus and Tyrannosaurus rex had sharp, pointed teeth for tearing flesh. If the dinosaur had powerful jaws, their teeth would be used for crushing their victim's bones. Triceratops used its toothless beak to gather up vegetation and its flat cheek teeth to chew tough plant material. Troodon snarled through serrated teeth, ideal for cutting through tough meat and sinews.

Mashed to a pulp

Gastroliths

The large herbivores had spoon-shaped or peg-like teeth designed for stripping plants. They didn't chew their food. Instead, the tough plant material was digested inside their huge guts. Many plant-eating dinosaurs swallowed gastroliths, or 'stomach stones', that helped to grind up the leaves and twigs.

No 9

Eocarcharia dinops

The fierce-eyed dinosaur Eocarcharia dinops used its huge and immensely hard brow-bone to butt rival males and attract potential mates. Its 7.6 cm (3 inch) long teeth were blade-shaped, just ideal for disabling live dinosaurs and severing their body parts! The top predator of its day, Eocarcharia's chief prey was the long-necked plant-eater, Nigersaurus.

Vital statistics

Name:	Eocarcharia (EE-oh-kahr-kar-ee-uh)
Meaning:	Dawn shark
Length:	6-8 m (19-26 ft)
Weight:	Up to1,600 kg (1.6 tonnes)
Diet:	Carnivorous
Time span:	112-99.6 mya
Period:	Cretaceous
Found:	Niger, North Africa

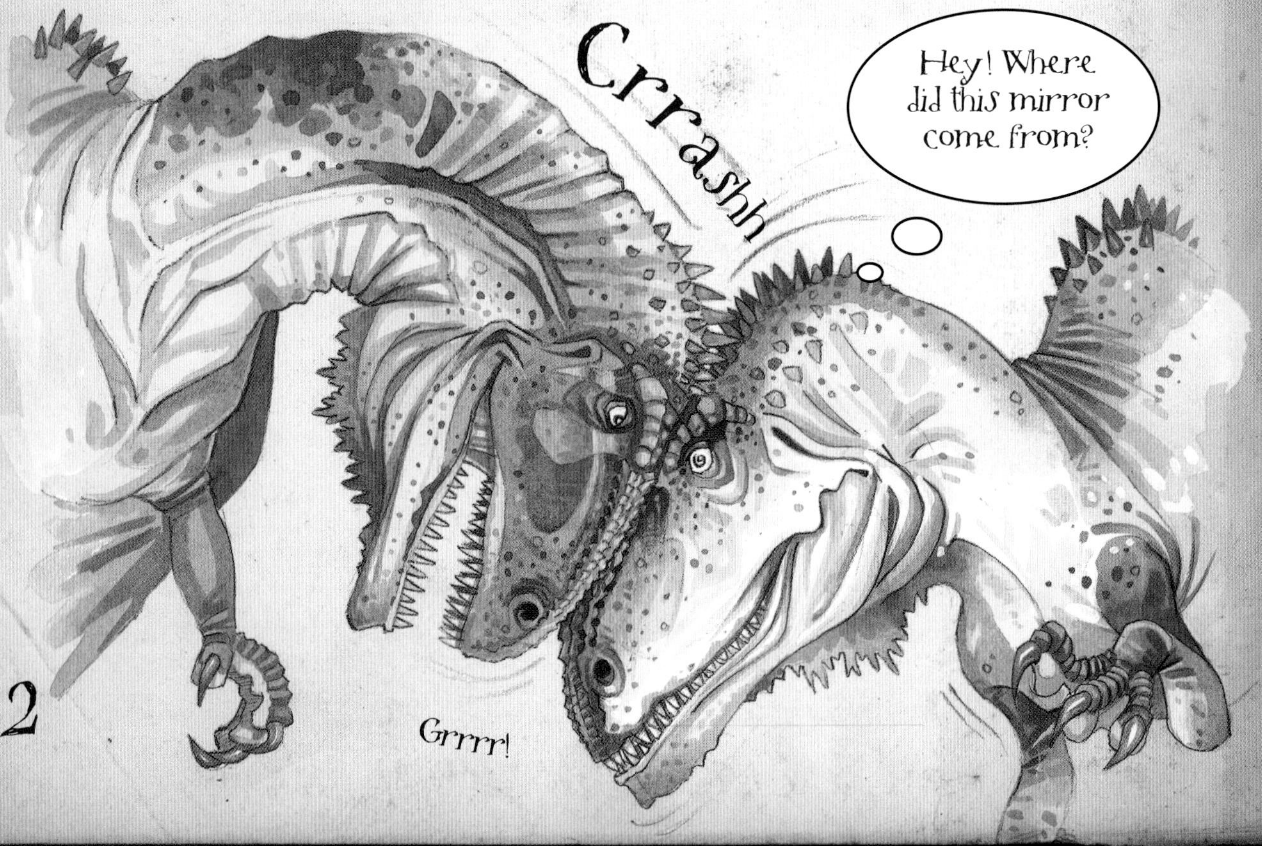

Crrashh

Hey! Where did this mirror come from?

Grrrr!

Be prepared! Always expect to read the very worst

Granddaddy dinosaur

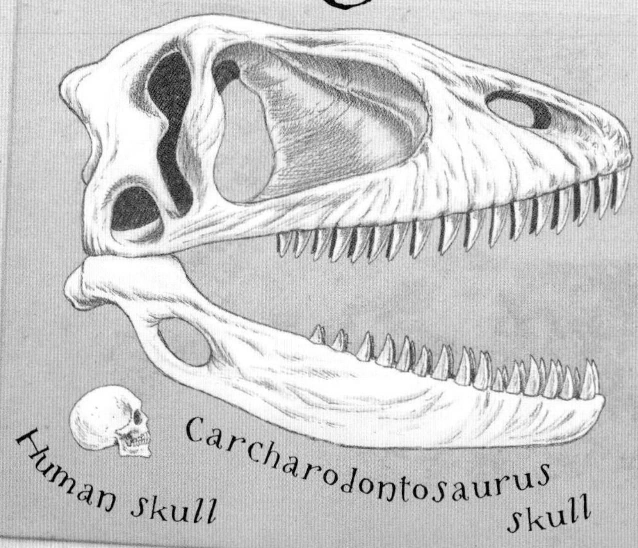

Over a long period of time, Eocarcharia dinops evolved into an even larger predator, Carcharodontosaurus. Carcharodontosaurus was a monstrous carnivore with a heavy-boned bulky body, and a massive tail. It grew up to 14 m (46 ft) long and weighed up to 15,000 kg (15 tonnes). When it reached full size its skull was as big as a fully-formed human!

Nigersaurus had a mouth shaped like the end of a vacuum cleaner. It ate vegetation from the ground like a modern cow.

Eocarcharia would have been too slow to run down most other dinosaurs. However, this deadly killer may have lain in wait and pounced on other dinosaurs when they weren't expecting it.

Nigersaurus

Munch!

Smack!

My mother always told me not to east fast food!

Triceratops

Although deceptively peaceful, Triceratops' long horns and strong body would have made it a formidable opponent for even an aggressive carnivore like Tyrannosaurus rex. Triceratops' head alone weighed a massive 455 kg (1,000 lb). When it charged to attack, Triceratops' 1.2 m (4 ft) long horns were capable of digging into the predator's flesh, even penetrating its heart. The solid bone attached to its skull shielded Triceratops' soft body from attack.

Vital statistics

Name:	Triceratops (tri-SERRA-tops)
Meaning:	Three-horned face
Length:	Up to 9 m (29 ft)
Weight:	6-12 tonnes
Diet:	Herbivorous
Time span:	67-65 mya
Period:	Late Cretaceous
Found:	USA

Be prepared! Always expect to read the very worst

Despite its small brain Triceratops was one of the most successful dinosaurs of the late Cretaceous Period. It was one of the last dinosaurs to have existed.

Horrible horns

Triceratops probably lived in small groups. The male with the largest and sharpest horns would be capable not just of defending its territory, but also of beating a rival male when it was time to mate.

Turning heads

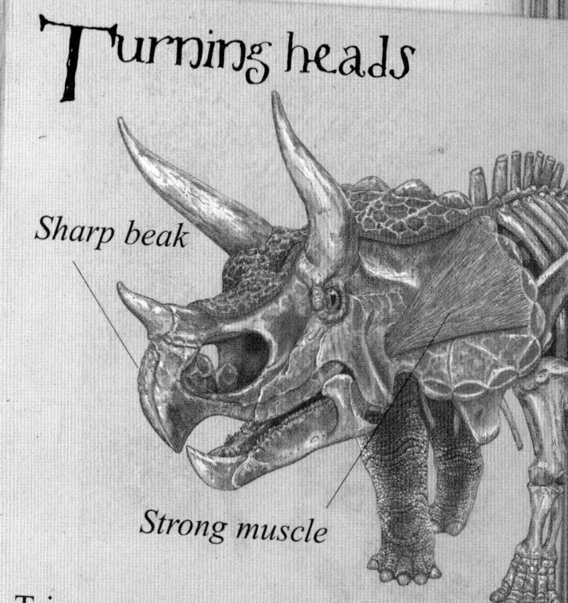

Triceratops had a special joint at the base of its skull, allowing it to move its head almost 360 degrees. In a fraction of a second it could position its head, ready to face a threatening predator.

Crrunch

No 7

Quetzalcoatlus

Quetzalcoatlus was one of the largest flying creatures to ever exist. This truly terrifying creature existed during the Cretaceous Period and, like the dinosaurs, was a reptile.

Quetzalcoatlus had hollow bones and a small, lightweight body. Its neck was 3 m (10 ft) long and its head and legs were each over 2.1 m (7 ft) in length.

Vital statistics

Name:	Quetzalcoatlus (KWET-zal-co-AT-lus), named after the Aztec god Quetzalcoatl
Wingspan:	Up to 12 m (39 ft)
Weight:	Up to 100 kg (220 lb)
Diet:	Carnivorous
Time span:	67-65 mya
Period:	Late Cretaceous
Found:	Texas, USA

Be prepared! Always expect to read the very worst

Eagle-eyed

The wings of Quetzalcoatlus were covered by a thin, leathery layer that stretched between its body, the top of its legs and its long fourth fingers. Claws protruded from the other fingers. It was able to soar vast distances and it had good eyesight, which it used to spot prey from the air. A flock of these incredible animals must have been an absolutely awesome sight!

Corpse-eater

Chomp!

What can I say? He had a lot of guts!

Quetzalcoatlus lived inland, near fresh-water lakes. It hunted fish by gliding over water using its long, toothless jaws to scoop up and filter its prey. Quetzalcoatlus was also a gruesome scavenger, walking on all fours in order to feed on the bodies of dead dinosaurs.

Although it wasn't technically a dinosaur itself, Quetzalcoatlus was a distant cousin to the dinosaurs. This huge flying reptile is included in this book because it was an incredibly scary creature.

No 6

Troodon

What made Troodon more frightening than other, larger, carnivorous dinosaurs, was its big brain and the ability to hunt at night, sometimes in packs. A group of hungry Troodon would be absolutely terrifying, eating just about anything they could slash and tear apart with their sharp teeth and huge, sickle-shaped toe claws.

Vital statistics

Name:	Troodon (TROH-oh-don)
Meaning:	Wounding tooth
Length:	Up to 2 m (6.5 ft)
Weight:	50 kg (110 lb)
Diet:	Carnivorous
Time span:	74-65 mya
Period:	Late Cretaceous
Found:	USA

Be prepared! Always expect to read the very worst

Brain box

An animal's intelligence is measured by EQ (encephalisation quotient). This is the size of the brain compared to the size of the body. The more of the body is taken up by the brain, the more intelligent the animal.

Massospondylus, an early herbivore, had a very low EQ and was one of the least intelligent dinosaurs. Whereas Troodon had one of the largest brains compared to the size of its body, and a higher EQ than any other dinosaur.

Massospondylus

Remember, boys – no growling or you'll give us away!

Stalk!

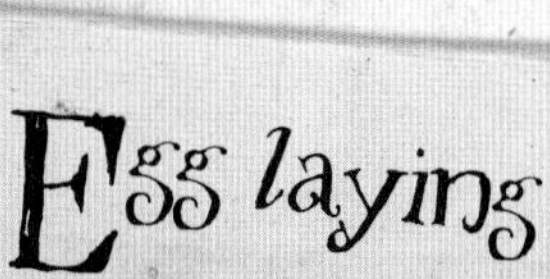

Egg laying

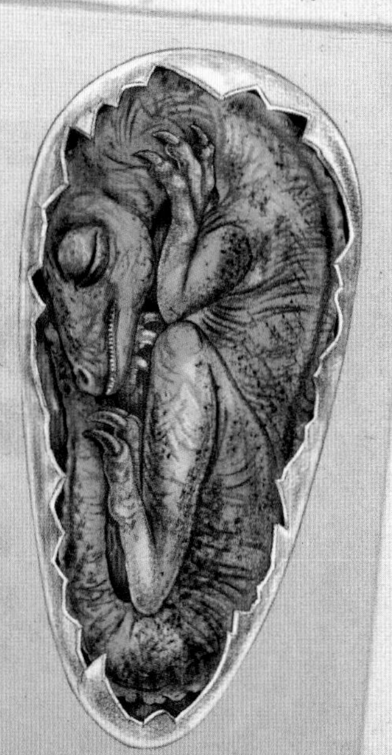

Female Troodons usually produced two eggs, which they incubated in earth nests. Like chickens, they often sat on the eggs, using their own body heat to warm them.

Night stalker

Troodon was only about the size of a human, so it was lightweight and able to run fast. A good sense of hearing and large, slightly forward-facing eyes allowed Troodon to pursue its prey in the dark.

Kronosaurus

An extremely scary marine reptile, Kronosaurus lived during the age of the dinosaurs. Kronosaurus was about the same size as a present-day sperm whale. Kronosaurus' sheer bulk meant it could eat almost any creature that swam past, including other marine reptiles, giant squid, large fish and probably the occasional unlucky dinosaur that passed too close to the shore.

Vital statistics

Name:	Kronosaurus (crow-no-SORE-us)
Meaning:	Titan lizard
Length:	Up to 12.5 m (41 ft)
Weight:	Up to 22 tonnes
Diet:	Carnivorous
Time span:	144-199 mya
Period:	Early Cretaceous
Found:	Australia

You wouldn't want to know this:

Kronosaurus is named after Kronos, the Greek god of time, who was so awful that he ate his own children.

Eeeeek!

And you just wanted to get your feet wet...

Sploosh!

Be prepared!
Always expect to read the very worst

Flipping fast

Kronosaurus' smooth body was driven through the water by four of the most powerful flippers ever developed by a marine animal. Capable of bursts of incredible speed, few creatures could escape it.

Big head!

This formidable predator had an enormous head, up to one third of the length of its body. Its strong jaws and 15 cm (6 inch) long teeth enabled it to crush the shells of giant turtles and large ammonites.

Giant squid

Car-sized turtle

Archelon was a huge turtle over 3.6 m (12 ft) long. A carnivore, Archelon probably ate jellyfish. When threatened by Kronosaurus it would have pulled its strong flippers into its thick protective shell.

Archelon

No 4

Allosaurus

The most successful carnivorous dinosaur of its time, Allosaurus was a fearsome, fast and agile hunter. Allosaurus had a short neck, a long tail and a massive skull with two blunt horns. Its jaws were lined with curved, dagger-like teeth, which had serrated edges like the blade of a steak knife. Allosaurus had strong talon-like claws on its hands and feet, enabling it to hold down and tear at its prey, which included large herbivorous dinosaurs such as Camptosaurus and Stegosaurus.

Well 'allo there!

Vital statistics

Name:	Allosaurus (AL-oh-saw-russ)
Meaning:	Other lizard
Length:	Up to 12 m (39 ft)
Weight:	Up to 4.5 tonnes
Diet:	Carnivorous
Time span:	153-135 mya
Period:	Late Jurassic
Found:	Tanzania and USA

Be prepared! Always expect to read the very worst

Childcare

Fossil evidence suggests that Allosaurus may have protected its children. It may have dragged dead carcasses back to its lair, feeding the young until they were fully grown, fending off any scavengers that might attack.

Vicious hunter

Allosaurus used its huge tail to help trap prey, and could tear the flesh off it whilst it was still alive! When the opportunity arose Allosaurus would scavenge for food, not only eating carcasses but also driving away smaller dinosaurs from their own kills.

Apatosaurus

Grrrr!

Growl!

Chomp!

Get off me, you big bullies!

Size doesn't matter

Even enormous dinosaurs like Apatosaurus and Diplodocus were not safe from attack. Hunting groups of Allosaurus would have brought down the weakest members picked from a herd of these monster herbivores.

No 3

Megaraptor

The fierce, bird-like dinosaur Megaraptor was incredibly deadly. This extreme predator had a lethal 35 cm (14 inch) long, sickle-shaped claw on each foot. Megaraptor had a curved neck and a huge head. Its immensely powerful jaws were armed with very sharp, serrated teeth. It was an intelligent dinosaur, so if Megaraptor hunted in packs it could probably kill any prey it wanted.

Despite its name, Megaraptor was not a raptor. Raptors were small to medium-sized carnivorous dinosaurs with large brains, two legs and hands that could grasp. You can find more information about these vicious dinosaurs on the opposite page.

Vital statistics

Name:	Megaraptor (meg-a-RAP-tor)
Meaning:	Huge robber
Length:	6-8 m (up to 26 ft)
Diet:	Carnivorous
Time span:	90-84 mya
Period:	Late Cretaceous
Found:	South America

Be prepared!
Always expect to read the very worst

Terrible claw

The raptor Deinonychus more than lived up to its name 'Terrible Claw'.

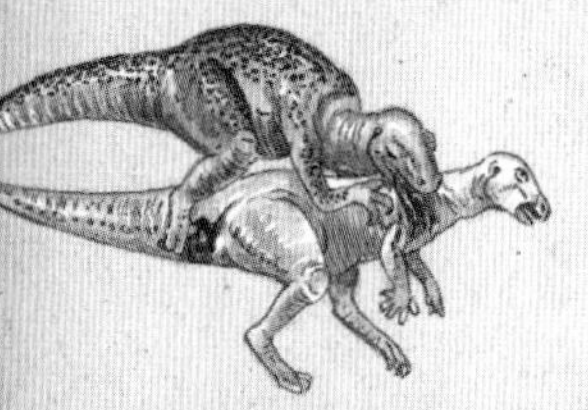

After chasing a similar-sized dinosaur like Hypsilophodon, Deinonychus overpowered its prey.

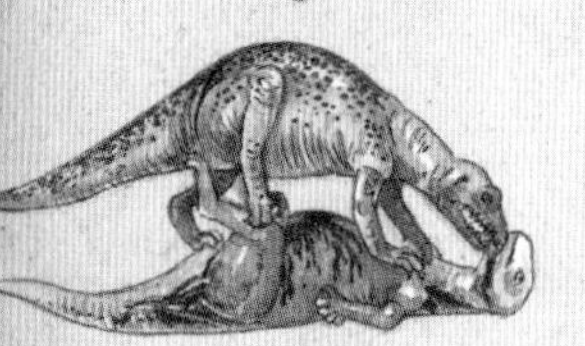

It tore open Hypsilophodon's body with its terrifying sharp-clawed fingers and sickle-like talons.

Speed kills

Utahraptor was one of the largest raptors that ever lived. Reaching speeds up to 100 kph (62 mph), these large-eyed raptors could spot and run down any prey they chose. As pack hunters, Utahraptors may have used one member as bait while the others caught and killed prey up to twice their size.

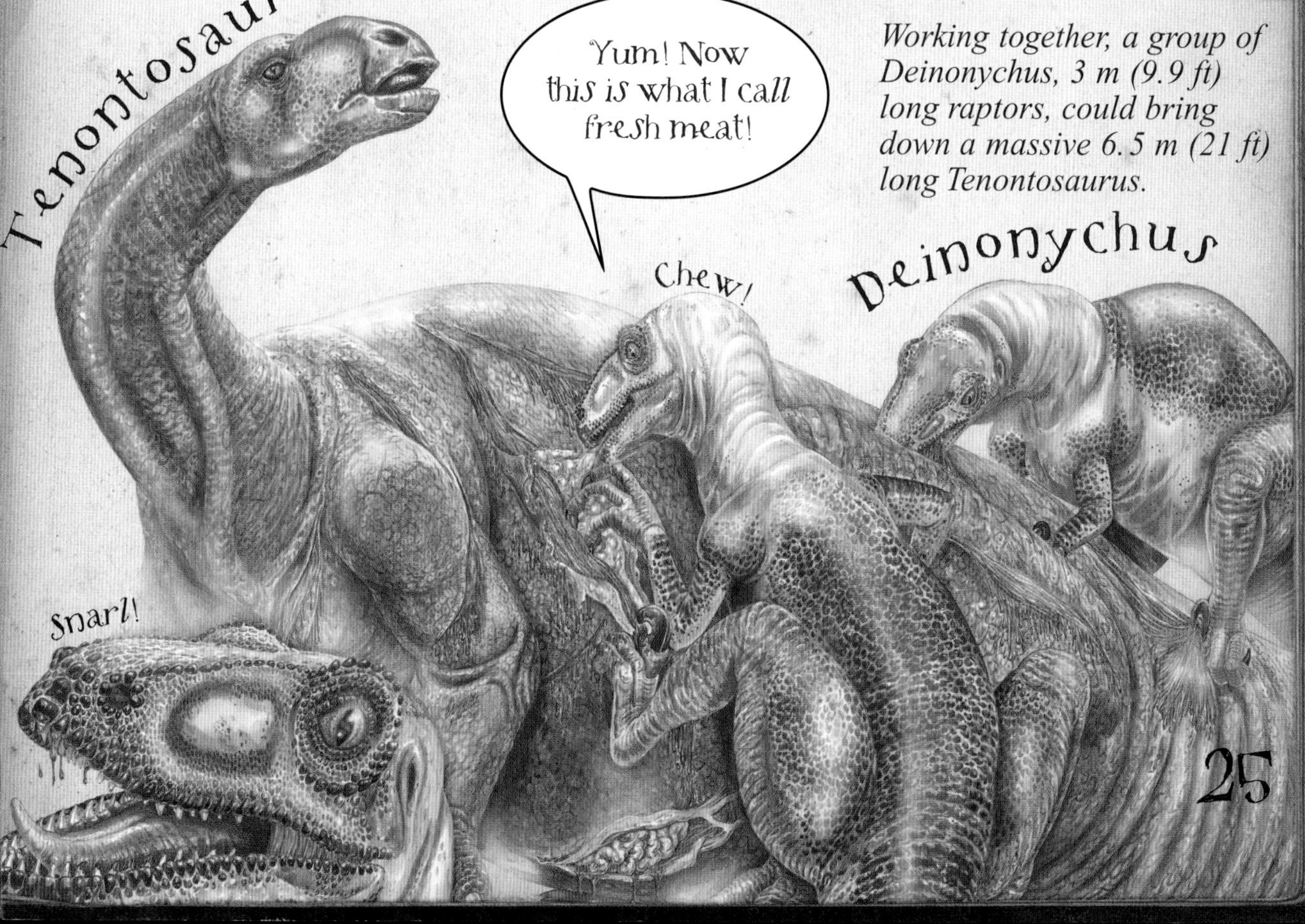

Tenontosaurus

Yum! Now this is what I call fresh meat!

Chew!

Deinonychus

Snarl!

Working together, a group of Deinonychus, 3 m (9.9 ft) long raptors, could bring down a massive 6.5 m (21 ft) long Tenontosaurus.

Top 10 Worst scary dinosaurs

Tyrannosaurus rex

Tyrannosaurus rex certainly was a fearsome dinosaur. This awesome carnivore had an enormous skull with massive 1.2 m (4 ft) long, muscular jaws packed with large, pointed teeth. It could run as fast as 24 kph (15 mph).

Tyrannosaurus rex had between 50 and 60 cone-shaped, saw-edged teeth for tearing flesh and crushing bones. They varied in size but the largest teeth were huge, up to 33 cm (13 inches) long including the root. Like most dinosaurs, Tyrannosaurus rex's teeth were replaceable. As teeth were lost or broken from fighting or eating, new teeth grew to replace them.

Vital statistics

Name:	Tyrannosaurus rex (tie-RAN-oh-sore-us rex)
Meaning:	Tyrant lizard king
Length:	Up to 13 m (42.6 ft)
Weight:	5-7 tonnes
Diet:	Carnivorous
Time span:	67-65 mya
Period:	Late Cretaceous
Found:	USA, Canada, East Asia

You wouldn't want to know this:

Tyrannosarus rex had an enormous, one metre wide open mouth which could rip apart a carcass with frightening ease. It could eat up to 230 kg (507 lb) of meat and bones in one bite!

Be prepared!

Always expect to read the very worst

Getting going

(a)

Tyrannosaurus probably rested on its stomach. However, because of its weight, getting up would have been a problem.

(b)

Tyrannosaurus may have used its small front legs for balance as it started to rise.

(c)

When its back legs were nearly straight it could throw its head back, using the momentum to lift itself off the ground.

(d)

Once fully upright Tyrannosaurus would be ready to set out in search of food.

What a pong!

Although Tyrannosaurus rex hunted alone, a heightened sense of smell helped it find dead flesh when there was little live meat around. Tyrannosaurus dismembered and ate the dead animal quickly: the stench of a rotting carcass would have attracted scavengers from far off. Albertosaurus and Daspletosaurus, which were both relatives of Tyrannosaurus, would have joined in the feast.

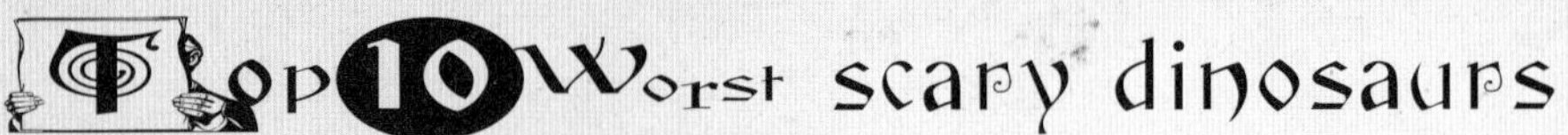

Spinosaurus

The largest carnivorous dinosaur that we know of was the extremely scary Spinosaurus, which could grow up to an amazing 18 m long!

This merciless dinosaur would attack and eat smaller prey of any kind, as well as scavenging from dead dinosaurs. Like a present-day crocodile, its long narrow snout contained jaws filled with short, sharp, straight teeth and its nostrils faced upwards. This meant that it was probably able to hunt sharks and other fish in nearby mangrove swamps.

Vital statistics

Name:	Spinosaurus (SPINE-oh-SORE-us)
Meaning:	Thorn lizard
Length:	Up to 18 m (59 ft)
Weight:	4-8 tonnes
Diet:	Carnivorous
Time span:	95-70 mya
Period:	Late Cretaceous
Found:	Egypt, Morocco

Be prepared!
Always expect to read the very worst

Dimetrodon, a fierce carnivore, lived nearly 200 million years before Spinosaurus. It too had a sail along its back. Dimetrodon was an early reptile, an ancestor to the mammals, called a pelycosaur.

Hot or cold?

The distinctive spines of the Spinosaurus grew up to 2 m (6.5 ft) long, with skin stretching between them like a sail. This sail made Spinosaurus appear larger and even more threatening to any rivals. Many scientists think that Spinosaurus also used its sail to manage its body temperature, rather like a radiator.

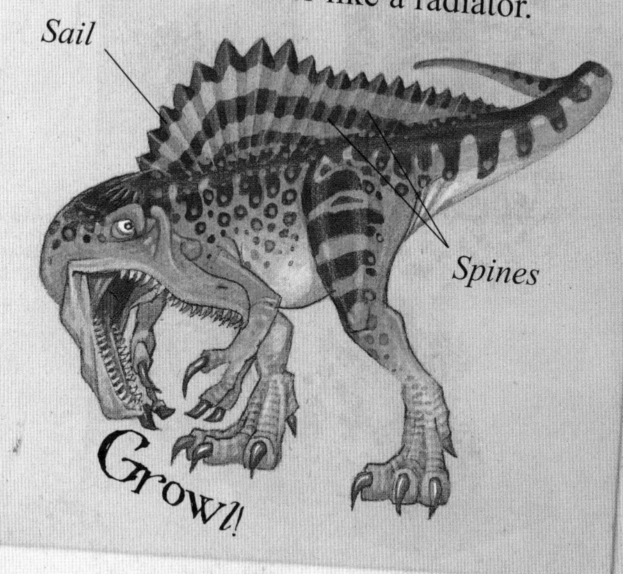

Little and large

Spinosaurus probably had the longest head of any known carnivorous dinosaur! Its mouth was nearly 2 m (6.5 ft) long. At the other end of the scale we have the Microraptor, which is the tiniest dinosaur ever discovered. At only 60 cm (2 ft) long, this bizarre dinosaur had two pairs of primitive wings – one set on its forearms and the other on its hind legs. The swift-moving Microraptor lived in trees and fed on insects.

Glossary

Ammonite Prehistoric, fast moving marine animal, closely related to the modern-day squid and octopus.

Amnion The thin membrane sac around the growing embryo.

Ancestor An early form of animal from which others evolved.

Bipedal Standing on two feet.

Carcass The body of a dead animal.

Carnivore A meat eater.

Coprolites Preserved dung.

Diet What an animal eats.

Digested Food that has been broken down by the body.

Embryo An animal developing inside an egg.

Evolve To develop into a different form.

Extinct No longer existing or living.

Fossilised Preserved in rock or as a rock.

Gastrolith A stone swallowed by dinosaurs to enable them to digest food in their stomachs by mashing the food up.

Habitat A plant or animal's natural place to live.

Herbivore A plant eater.

Incubated Kept at a particular temperature.

Lethal Deadly.

Mammal An animal that gives birth to live young and suckles them.

Mangrove A tropical tree growing beside water, having roots that begin above ground.

Marine Living in the sea.

Mesozoic Era A period of time which started 225 million years ago and ended 65 million years ago.

Omnivore An animal that eats a variety of food including meat and plants.

Overpower To overcome by being stronger.

Palaeontologist A person who studies prehistoric life.

Pelycosaur A type of prehistoric animal.

Predator An animal that kills and eats other animals.

Prehistoric The period long ago before written records were made.

Prey An animal hunted by a predator.

Primitive At an early stage of evolution.

Reptile A cold-blooded vertebrate that breathes air and has skin covered with scales.

Scavenger An animal that searches for decaying flesh for food.

Serrated Saw-like. Having a row of sharp or tooth-like projections.

Sickle A type of curved knife.

Sinew A tough band of tissue that usually connects muscle to bone.

Supercontinent In prehistoric times, a single, immense mass of land consisting of all the modern continents before they broke apart.

Talon A sharp claw.

Index